Let's Get Creative with Quilt Labels

Shannon Gingrich Shirley

Schiffer Publishing Ltd

4880 Lower Valley Road • Atglen, PA 19310

Dedicated to three very special people in my life...

To **Mary Kerr** and **Kristin Stolte**
You both have been so patient and kind with me. You are wise and trusted; you have offered me advice and guidance. I appreciate your enthusiasm; it has been motivational for me. I couldn't have better mentors and coaches. Most of all, I appreciate your friendship.
Thank you from the bottom of my heart.

To **Judy Hall**
For working with me to claim the second half of my life. The time I spent with you was life changing.
Thank you!

Copyright © 2013 by Shannon Gingrich Shirley

Library of Congress Control Number: 2013953965

"Schiffer," "Schiffer Publishing, Ltd. & Design," and the "Design of pen and inkwell" are registered trademarks of Schiffer Publishing, Ltd.

Designed by Molly Shields
Type set in Dakota/NewBskvll BT

ISBN: 978-0-7643-4472-5
Printed in China

Published by Schiffer Publishing, Ltd.
4880 Lower Valley Road
Atglen, PA 19310
Phone: (610) 593-1777; Fax: (610) 593-2002
E-mail: Info@schifferbooks.com

For our complete selection of fine books on this and related subjects, please visit our website at www.schifferbooks.com. You may also write for a free catalog.

This book may be purchased from the publisher. Please try your bookstore first.

We are always looking for people to write books on new and related subjects. If you have an idea for a book, please contact us at proposals@schifferbooks.com

Schiffer Publishing's titles are available at special discounts for bulk purchases for sales promotions or premiums. Special editions, including personalized covers, corporate imprints, and excerpts can be created in large quantities for special needs. For more information, contact the publisher.

Contents

Introduction

Since 1988, quilting has been my passion. For many years I was self taught, so most of my early quilts do not have labels on them. At some point, I remember being told to label my quilts with at least my name and the dates I completed them. When you make a quilt, you believe you will always remember when you made it, but, as with everything we do, those memories get fuzzy. The labels I made at first were very basic; making them was just a boring chore.

Over the years, I began to realize that many of the quilts I made had stories that I wanted to stay with the quilt—not just *when* I made it, but *who* I made it for, or the reason I chose the specific colors. Possibly it was a challenge quilt and I wanted to remember what the challenge was. Maybe it was to celebrate a certain event in someone's life. Sometimes it was a quilt I'd started in a class with a particular instructor. These are all part of the quilt's story. It is important that this information stay with the quilt so others will know the provenance of the quilt in the future.

April 14th - Reach as High as You Can Day!
by Shannon Shirley, Virginia, May 2012

Today is the day to reach for the stars, dream big!
Believe in yourself, make a plan and go for it.
Reach as high as you can and turn your dream into a reality!

www.onceinarabbitmoon.com
www.facebook.com/onceinarabbitmoon

At first, I started adding just a little bit of decoration to my very basic labels, but as time progressed, I became more creative. I began making different shaped labels, using a variety of edge treatments, and designing them to coordinate with the quilts. It became more than just a chore to create a label; I had fun coming up with new ideas. Now, don't get me wrong; I would still prefer not to have to label my quilts, but now I enjoy the process more. I love learning the stories connected to the quilts I see. Every quilt deserves to have a label on it recording its story!

In this book, I will share a variety of labels I have made and the quilts that inspired them. I will also share the techniques and materials used, so that you can start getting creative with your own quilt labels.

Chapter 1

Basic Labels: Why Add More?

The label on the left is one of the early labels that I made using a permanent fabric pen and muslin. It was made for the pinwheel wall hanging on the right and certainly identifies when it was made and by who made it, but there is much more to the story of this quilt. This quilt connects three generations in a simple way, but that connection will eventually be lost without a more detailed label.

At this point in my quilting I realized that everything I had made had been given away, so *This One Is For Me* was made for me to keep. I used some of each of the cotton prints in my stash to create the 72 pinwheels. Many of the fabrics were scraps from dresses that I had sewn for my girls and projects I had made to use in our first home. Seventy-two different buttons from my mum's button box embellish the centers of each pinwheel. I hand-quilted inside each pinwheel; I also hand-quilted a detailed pattern in the border. This is the largest hand-quilting project I've made. One of the stories I like to share about this quilt is having to scrounge around to find 144 fabrics. If I made a quilt now using some of each cotton print that I have in my stash, it would be enormous!

Every quilt doesn't have a detailed story, but even a short story is worth recording. Think about recording some of that information on the label so that it won't be lost in the future.

Edna's Quilt was made from a collection of orphan blocks that I purchased from a vendor at a quilt show. If I had just labeled this with my name and the date I made it, someone might think that I had pieced the blocks myself.

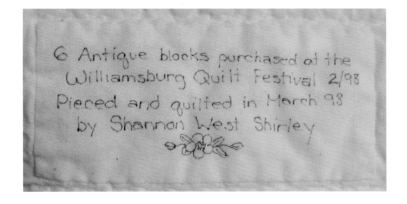

I made this quilt for my brother and his wife as a Christmas gift. As you can see, I decided to add my maiden name, probably because it would show the connection to Tyler and Margaret.

Many of my early labels have simple drawings on them to coordinate them to the quilt top.

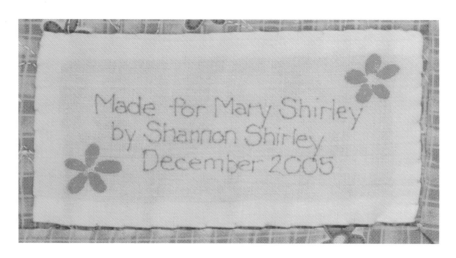

There are probably four people on this earth who might remember this little quilt's story.

My niece Rebecca Shirley, who was seven at the time, made my daughter Jenny Shirley a poetry book as a gift for her fourteenth birthday. This particular poem was Rebecca's mom's favorite. I should have included this information on the label. For Christmas 2005, I recreated the poem and drawing in fabric and fabric marker for Mary Shirley. I chose to keep this label simple and embellished it with flowers similar to those on the border fabric.

Tickled Pink? was made using the leftover half-square triangles from another quilt named *Baby Blue*. At the time, I was practicing adding multiple borders to my quilts. In June of 2001, I worked on hand-quilting this wall hanging while my dad was in the hospital undergoing surgery for a tumor that turned out to be Castleman's disease. Even though we were first told it was Lymphoma, I wasn't sure if we were tickled pink over the results we were given.

Recording when an event takes place, even if it isn't necessarily the happiest of events, can be useful in the future. My mum and I could not remember when my dad had undergone this surgery, but the label told us.

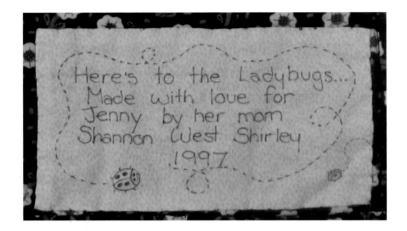

One very important point to remember is to give credit to the designer or company whose pattern you use, even if it's an adaptation.

Back when I made this quilt for my youngest daughter Jenny, I was just labeling it with what I knew should be there. Now I know that I left some very important information off of this label. For the record, this quilt is an adaptation of *Here's to the Bears* from *Little Quilts All Through The House* by Alice Berg, Mary Ellen Von Holt, and Sylvia Johnson, published by That Patchwork Place.

This particular quilt was made from a kit that my mum bought at The Mid-Atlantic Quilt Festival. In the rush of completing it for a Christmas gift, I never thought about recording the information of the pattern name or the vendor where the kit was bought.

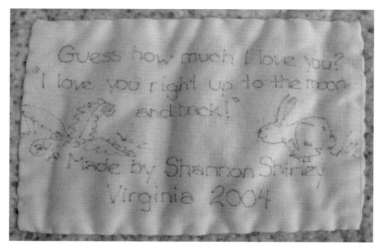

This label belongs with the quilt on the opposite page on the left, which is finished. The quilt on the right has not been quilted, but was pieced in 2004. Both of these quilts deserve labels with more information on them for a number of reasons. First, they were inspired by the fabric in the centers of each of the stars. *Guess How Much I Love You* is a book written by Sam McBratney and illustrated by Anita Jeram. When I saw this fabric, I just had to make a quilt. I chose a variety of prints and colors that I liked with the novelty print and started by fussy cutting as many squares on point as I could. I had enough squares to design two quilts, but because I don't like anything to be exactly the same, I chose to make one with white background blocks and one with multi-colored nine patches. Including this information, and that they are one of two and two of two, is important to me. When I finish the second one, I will make new labels.

Something to think about: If your quilt is stolen, the label can be removed with very little effort. Consider using a thick permanent fabric marker to write your name on the back of your quilts before adding the labels over the top. You also can add the label to the back of the quilt before quilting it, but then you are quilting through the words and I choose not to do that.

Labels can be meaningful, helpful, or just interesting. In the following chapters, I will share a variety of labels I have made and the quilts that inspired them, starting with some of my early most basic labels and progressing to much more detailed examples. I will also share the various products and techniques I used to create these labels.

I hope that these labels will inspire you to tell *your* quilt's story!

Chapter 2

Squares and Rectangles

A very simple label may be all that you need. This label identifies that I did not make the tablecloth. It explains that there was damage that I covered with the baskets, and that I added the border and machine quilted it. I could have chosen to go into more detail, but didn't need to.

If I made this label again, I would use a double layer of white material so the orange backing fabric wouldn't show through the label.

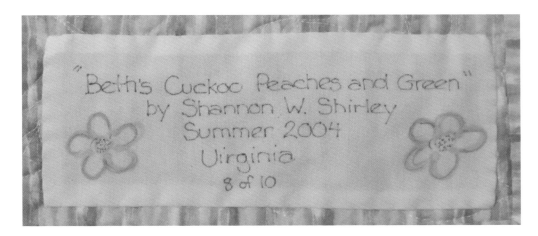

This label shares the title of the quilt, who made it, and when it was made, along with the state, and "8 of 10", which tells us that it is part of a series. What it doesn't tell you it that I purchased some blocks, strips, and other fabric pieces from Beth Wiesner at our guild's annual yard sale. The name of her pattern company is Cuckoo Quilts. For the $25 that I spent, I managed to make ten quilts of varying sizes by only adding minimal fabric. It took me two weeks to piece all ten items and I ended up with about a dozen leftover pieces. It was a personal challenge to see if I could use it all up. I had a great time and I thought Beth was cuckoo for selling all of it, so each quilt name in the series starts with "Beth's Cuckoo."

I have a collection of nativities, so this embroidery pattern was too cute to pass up. I love doing hand embroidery because it is very relaxing and is easily transportable. I like trying new techniques on small projects, so for this project I decided to add an on-point postage stamp border. I love the way it looks, but I don't think I'll ever use that border technique again. However, seven years later, I can't really remember why I felt that way—so you never know; maybe I will try it again someday! If I had included the title of the book I used to design the border, making this border again would be much easier.

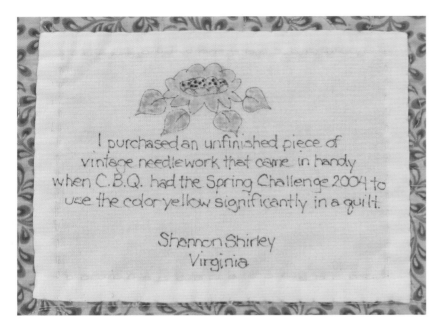

I purchased an unfinished piece of vintage needlework that came in handy when C.B.Q. had the Spring Challenge 2004 to use the color yellow significantly in a quilt.

Shannon Shirley
Virginia

This quilt was inspired by an unfinished vintage piece of linen and a guild challenge to use yellow significantly in a quilt. I finished the embroidery and added the green leaves and scrappy border. I doodled one of the flowers from the quilt top on the label. The backing fabric shows through the label however, so I added a running stitch to give the appearance of quilting around the label. It almost makes the white seam allowance look like a border around the rest of the label.

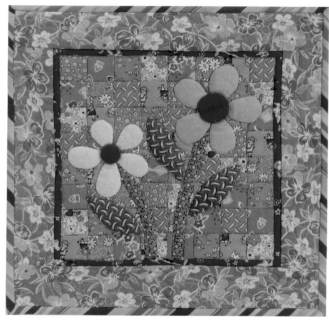

I belong to the Quilt Professionals Network (QPN). In March of 2008, we were given a yellow and white vintage block and challenged to use it in a 12" x 12" mini quilt. Mary Kerr had written the information on a business card, which she attached to the block. I traced the information and the outline of the card onto the label and added the quilt's name, my name, and where and when it was made. The quilt was made using reproduction prints except for the border, which is a vintage feed sack. This detail, along with Mary's name, should have been included in the label.

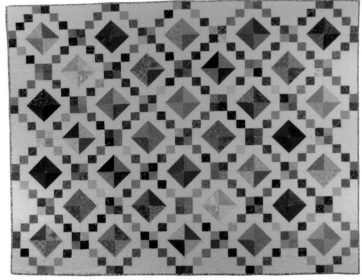

I started this quilt top in a class I took October 21, 2001. I finished the top for my guild's Winter 2004 Challenge, which was to start or finish a scrap quilt. I quilted it in January 2005, just in time to turn it in for the Cabin Branch Quilters (CBQ) quilt show. This was the first full-size quilt I quilted on my HQ-16 mid-arm machine. All the appropriate information is included on this label. The pattern is Jewel Box and the name of the quilt is *Just In Time*. If I had added a bit more color with some kind of embellishments, it would put the label over the top!

Just wanting to get a label on this piece, I made a square label, traced the information onto it using a permanent fabric pen, and then decorated it with a variety of soft undulating curves using permanent fabric markers. This quilt was made in the first class I ever took at a national show. It was definitely the beginning of my introduction to art quilts and unlearning all the rules I had been teaching myself.

The word I remember most from this class is "undulating" and the curves on the label are a reminder of that. Maybe I should have named it Undulating Tulips instead!

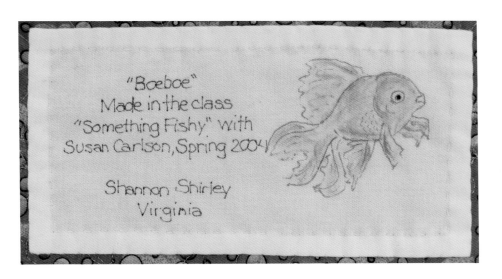

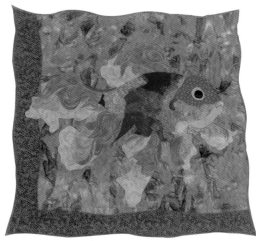

When my guild invited Susan Carlson to lecture and teach a workshop, I knew I was signing up. I was curious about how all the art quilts I had been seeing were made and wanted to begin to learn new techniques. I decided not to use one of Susan's patterns because I am not that fond of fish and if I was going to make a fish quilt, I was going to make a quilt of my oldest daughter's pet oranda goldfish, Boeboe! I should add that it was inspired by a photograph and that it is an original design.

This quilt was inspired by the book *Sunbonnet Sue Gets It All Together At Home* by Jean Ray Laury. I chose to write this information around the edge of the label because the main purpose of the wall hanging was a thank you for my mum, who helps me so much with all sorts of things that make my life easier. In our home, she is also known as the Laundry Fairy because she can remove just about any stain and brighten dingy linens like magic. (She uses many different products and techniques and I embroidered their brand names in a multi-colored border before completing the quilt with a scrappy binding.) I wish I had made two labels: one of which would have highlighted and acknowledged the source of inspiration and the other with the thank you to my mum.

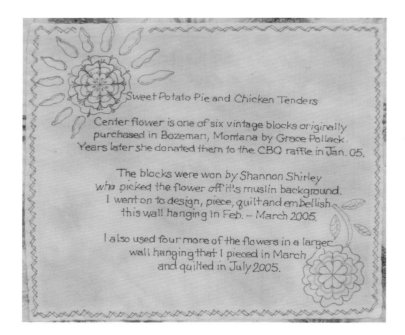

Sweet Potato Pie and Chicken Tenders

Center flower is one of six vintage blocks originally purchased in Bozeman, Montana by Grace Pollack. Years later she donated them to the CBQ raffle in Jan. 05.

The blocks were won by Shannon Shirley who picked the flower off it's muslin background. I went on to design, piece, quilt and embellish this wall hanging in Feb. – March 2005.

I also used four more of the flowers in a larger wall hanging that I pieced in March and quilted in July 2005.

Sweet Potato Pie and Chicken Tenders was inspired by the center flower block, which was one of six that I won at my quilt guild's annual silent auction. The only things I would do differently on this label would be to use a double layer of white, so that the backing fabric didn't show through the label and I would name the other quilt I made, not just reference it. However, at this point, I had been having so much fun making shaped labels that I would probably have made a colored label shaped like the original flower appliqué.

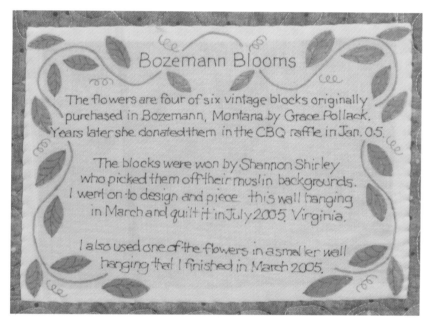

Bozemann Blooms

The flowers are four of six vintage blocks originally purchased in Bozemann, Montana by Grace Pollack. Years later she donated them in the CBQ raffle in Jan. 05.

The blocks were won by Shannon Shirley who picked them off their muslin backgrounds. I went on to design and piece this wall hanging in March and quilt it in July 2005. Virginia.

I also used one of the flowers in a smaller wall hanging that I finished in March 2005.

This quilt was made with four of six blocks that I won at my quilt guild's annual silent auction. I chose to decorate this label with leaves and vines similar to that of the quilt top. Being almost a pair of quilts, I would say the same things about the label on *Bozemann Blooms* that I said for *Sweet Potato Pie and Chicken Tenders*.

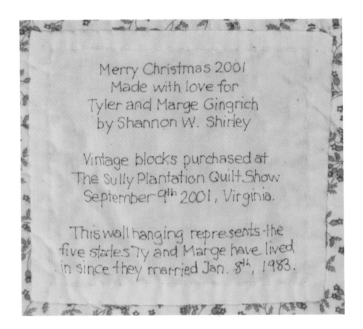

If you read the label, you might wonder which was the fifth state my brother and his wife lived in because there are only four state blocks. When I purchased the vintage blocks, there wasn't a Virginia block available, so I represented the fifth state by appliquéing the dogwood blossoms in the four corners and embroidering Virginia near one of the dogwood blossoms. I could have included this information on the label. Again, I need to point out that a simple label with all the pertinent information is good. But why shouldn't the label be just as special as the quilt? A dogwood shaped label would have been much more interesting.

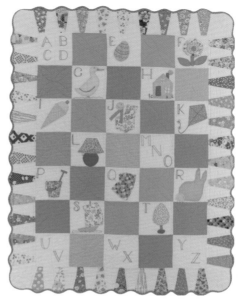

A green border of the binding fabric would be a nice addition to this label just to frame it out and set if off from the backing fabric or I could have blanket stitched around the edge in green. The wording on the label is fairly clear, but I could have said that "Shannon West Shirley designed the layout using the vintage pieces as inspiration and Jill Green Gingrich hand-quilted it." Also, during the design process, my mum found the original pattern reprinted in a magazine and we used that pattern to create some of the missing blocks, but not all of them because we liked the layout that I had designed. Recording the history of the original design is very important, so I will be adding another label to this quilt very soon.

This is the second of six wall quilts created
for Mary Kerr's 2 year challenge.
Every 4 months we receive a vintage
quilt block and can do anything we want
to it as long as it appears in some way on
the front of the finished 24" x 24" wall quilt.

Made by Shannon Shirley
2811 Noble Fir Court
Woodbridge, Virginia

Nov. 06 ~ March 07

THE MEDITERRANIAN! · BARCELONA
CIVITAVECCHIA · TARQUINIA · LIVORNO
MARSEILLE · CASSIS · NAPLES · CAPRI
VILLEFRANCHE · NICE · EZE · OCT. 2006

France   Italy
Spain
Mediterranean
Sea
October 20 - 28
2006

Before anyone notices, yes I spelled *Mediterranean* incorrectly on the front of my quilt and it took three years for anyone to notice! I did, however, spell it correctly on the embroidery I stitched while on an awesome cruise with a very dear friend who has since passed away. So this quilt is very special to me, spelling mistake and all! There are two labels on this quilt, one about the cruise and one about the challenge I was participating in at the time.

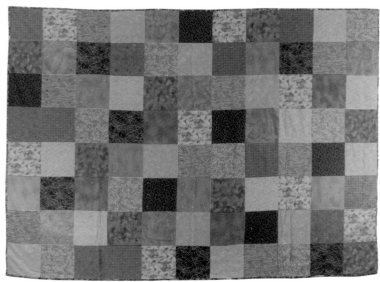

Very simple labels can often suit the quilt for which they are created. My daughter, Emma, who was eleven at the time, wanted just large plain squares. She would have preferred solid colored fabrics, but I couldn't bring myself to work with solids at the time. This was before I could machine quilt and I wasn't going to attempt hand-quilting anything of this size, so I tied it nine times in each square. The label incorporates some of the colors from the quilt and I believe was fused down before I added blanket stitching. I redid the stitching recently and you will see the original later in the book along with directions on how to avoid my mistake.

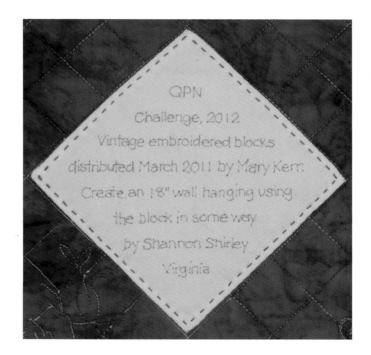

This is another great example of a very simple label that suits the quilt for which it was made. The original vintage embroidered block is appliquéd on point on the front of the wall hanging. The label I created was also set on point to resemble the original block. I used a royal blue permanent pen to coordinate with the blue batik fabric and accented it with a running stitch of green floss similar to that of the green batik leaves.

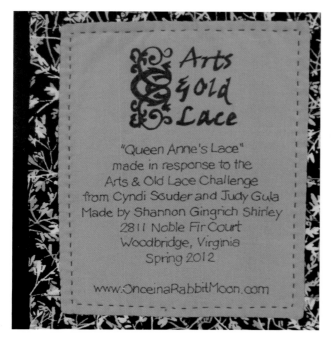

Tracing the logo from the challenge that I was participating in added interest to this label. Making a shaped label for this wall hanging would not have suited it because there was no solid, defined shape that I could have used. Again, I used the running stitch a quarter-inch in from the edge. I like how it secures the label to the quilt and adds a bit of texture and detail.

First, I made a simple square label for this quilt. I had imagined that I would blanket stitch it down or add a black running stitch around the edge. Instead, I recreated a design element from the front of the quilt by fusing small pieces of black material onto the label and free motion stitching them into place before I sewed the label on the back of the quilt.

Chapter 3

Circles and Ovals

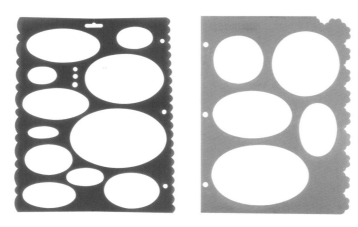

Circular labels suit the theme or design of some quilts, but I would have to say that my favorite easy-to-make label is an oval. I think they are pleasing shapes that look great on most quilts.

For most of my small circle and oval labels, I use some old stencils leftover from when my girls were little. Although most of the shapes are too small for labels, the larger ones are the perfect size.

For circular labels, I often draw around lids or plates in various sizes. When making rectangular and square labels, I use my Plexiglas quilt rulers to draw them the size I want. Ovals have always been a bit more difficult to draw so, for your convenience, I have included a series of graduated shapes that you can trace for making labels. *(See pages 153 - 159)*

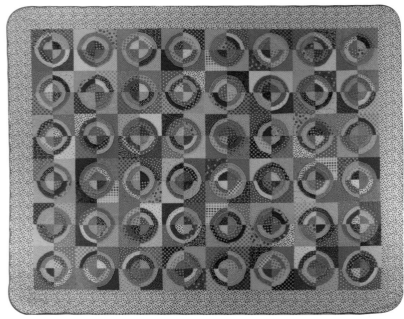

Seeing Spots and the next two quilts were made from fabrics that had dots and spots all over them. I had always wanted to make a raw edge quilt like this and the collection of spotted fabrics I had seemed like the perfect choice for this project. While the blocks were hanging on my design wall, two of my daughters expressed a desire to have it be their quilt. A circular label was an obvious choice. This label would look great with an accent of blanket or outline stitching around the edge. Making a raw edge, circular label would have been perfect!

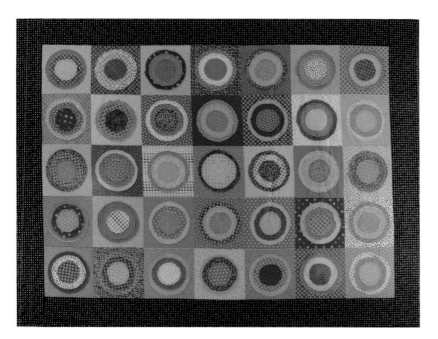

Spring 2005

Going
by Dotty!

Shannon Shirley

Virginia

Having plenty of polka dot material leftover, I sewed another collection of blocks. Right before I cut them into quarters like the first quilt, one of my daughters said she liked them the way they were. I found another dotted material for the border and one for the back, and again added a circular label.

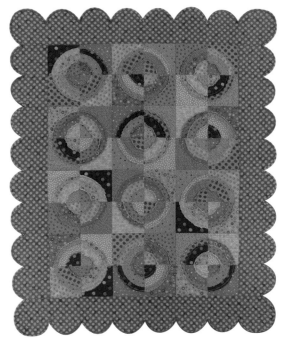

While teaching at a local shop, I needed a smaller sample of this design for them to display, so I sewed a baby quilt. Since it was similar to *Seeing Spots*, it only seemed right to name it *Seeing Baby Spots*. The three quilts seemed like a series, so I decided it needed to have a matching label. All of these labels could benefit from an accent of embroidery around the edge of the labels to make them stand out even more!

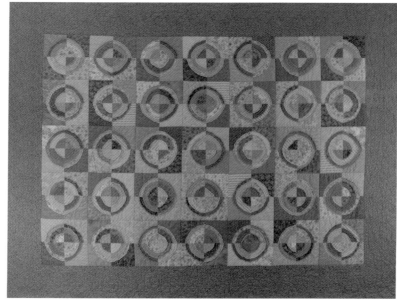

During one of the classes I taught, I started making these blocks. Every time my mum would see them, she expressed her love of the collection of colors. For Mother's Day that year I gave her the quilt top, but didn't finish the quilt for almost another year. My life was spinning around me at the time, so I named it *Spinning Wheels*. I wrote the label around and around instead of in straight lines because it suited how I was feeling and the name I had chosen for the quilt.

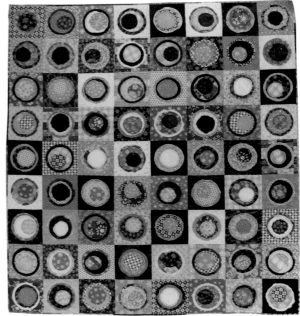

For years I had been collecting fabric in blue and white snowy prints. Wanting a fun and easy project to work on, I settled on the raw edge technique again. The whole circles seemed like snowballs. I offset the circles as I sewed a more random look. While working on this project during the winter of 2009-2010, we had two huge blizzards, and that's how the quilt got its name. With all the texting going on at the time, "snOMG" was frequently used in communicating about the amount of snow we had. Again, it only seemed right to use a circular snowball label on this quilt.

Looking at these two pictures side by side; I think the obvious choice for this label would have been a square set on point. I love rick rack, so I would still use that to frame the label because it is a design element from the front of the quilt.

Free To Be Me! could have had any shape of label on it, but I was in a hurry and I was making two labels at the same time for the same challenge. It was a very colorful quilt, so I chose to add blanket stitch using two strands of variegated floss. I like the frame it gives the label and it makes it seem more secure, even though someone could pick out all the stitching and remove it if they really wanted to.

Anything Is Possible! was another obvious choice for a circular label. Using blue and red permanent fabric pens for the text was a simple way to coordinate the label with the quilt. The space at the top bothered me, so I decided to add a double star button tied on with embroidery floss like the buttons on the front of the quilt. To finish it off, I did a running stitch around the outer edge of the label using six strands of floss. When you do this running stitch, you need to be careful not to stitch through to the front of the quilt. I like to stitch into the batting because it gives the label texture like it has been quilted.

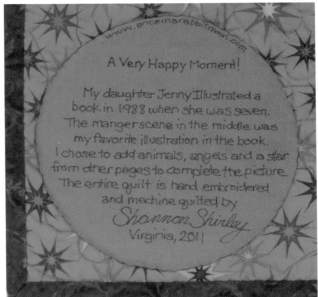

Short on time again, I used my go-to easy circular label, although a shaped label would have suited this quilt. After all the time that went into it, I could have spent a little more time on the label. A yellow star, a holly leaf, or maybe even an angel would have been more interesting, and a pleasant surprise when the quilt was turned over.

This label was inspired by the fabric used in the binding and borders. The fabric looks like the circles on a penny rug and they even have what looks like blanket stitch on them.

45

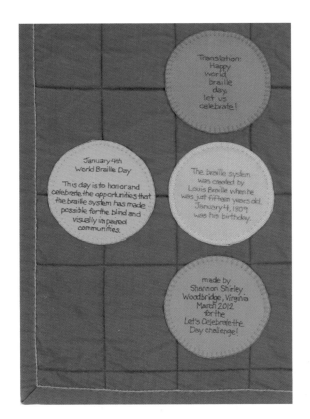

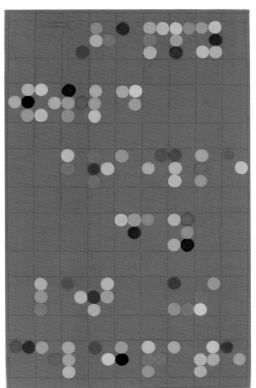

A collection of dots makes up not only the quilt, but also the label. The four dots of the label represent the letter "W" in braille for World Braille Day, which this wall hanging was made to celebrate. The quilt says, "Happy world braille day, let us celebrate."

Permanent fabric markers and a permanent fabric pen were used to create this simple yet attractive label. Doodling flowers and leaves similar to those in the backing fabric coordinated the label very well. Now that I've said that, you probably didn't notice that the flowers are not evenly spaced because I did not preplan their layout. I just jumped in and got it done. So if that detail will bother you, take the time to layout the design on paper first.

This particular label is another example of a simple oval, decorated with some doodles from elements of the quilt that are quite suitable for this wall hanging.

Rick rack is a design element from the quilt which sets the label off from the backing fabric and accents the spider.

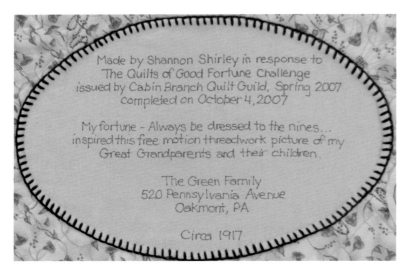

Made by Shannon Shirley in response to
The Quilts of Good Fortune Challenge
issued by Cabin Branch Quilt Guild, Spring 2007
completed on October 4, 2007

My fortune - Always be dressed to the nines...
inspired this free motion threadwork picture of my
Great Grandparents and their children.

The Green Family
520 Pennsylvania Avenue
Oakmont, PA

Circa 1917

Because the picture on the front of this quilt is framed in brown and accented with a darker brown, I decided to add some brown around the edge of the label to frame it out. After trying a vintage upholstery trim that was too wide and overpowered the label, I considered going to the store to find a smaller trim, but decided to use the floss that I had on hand to blanket stitch around the edge of the label.

Many of the fabrics used in this quilt have musical notes on them. The recipient was the director of The Prince William County Youth Orchestra and a musician herself. I chose to doodle musical notes around the edge of this label, but not being a musician myself, I just made them up. When I gave the quilt to Carol, she laughed when she noticed my "mistake."

I like the oval label just fine, however, I probably should have sewn the running stitch instead of just drawing it. I like the texture that stitching gives the label. A spool of thread block would have made a good label for this quilt, with the words written in the square that represents the thread. If the background of the spool block matched the backing on the quilt, it would blend in and the spool would stand out.

This quilt was made by recreating artwork that my daughter, Emma, drew when she was in preschool and elementary school. With all the cat drawings on this quilt, the label had to have paw prints on it.

Framing out this label with a row of outline stitch in six strands of orange embroidery floss coordinates it to the design element of the orange accent border on the front of the quilt.

As you have seen, basic shapes can make some great labels. Next, we are going to look at shaped theme labels which can be quite fun to design and not much more difficult to make.

Chapter 4

Shaped Theme Labels

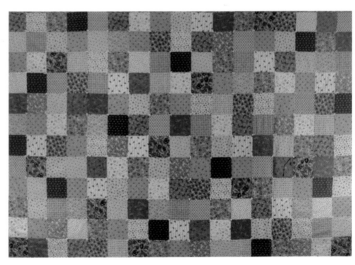

This was the first shaped label I made. It was an obvious choice for this ladybug quilt: every fabric used in this quilt is a ladybug print including the binding. Using two strands of red floss, I blanket stitched around the edge and then outline stitched the legs in black. The rest of the label was drawn with a permanent fabric pen.

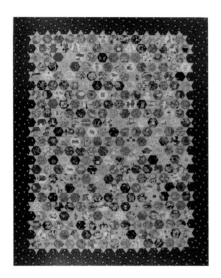

The first week of February 2003, I was piecing rows for this quilt when I ran across a fussy cut hexagon of the Space Shuttle *Columbia*. Just days earlier, on February 1, the *Columbia* had disintegrated on reentry to the earth's atmosphere. I decided to date that hexagon with a permanent fabric marker. Maybe I should add another hexagon label in memory of the seven crew members who were lost.

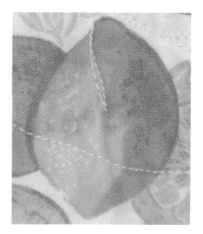

The theme of this quilt inspired the label: "If life gives you lemons, make a lemonade quilt." I traced and enlarged a lemon from the backing fabric to create the shape. This label not only records information about who made the quilt and when, but also the challenge that the quilt was made for and the quote that inspired it. Additionally, it records a suggestion made by my daughter after the quilt was completed. This was quite a bit of information to put on this label, so it was a big lemon!

Red White and Blue Sue! was created using the vintage block on the right. The label I made for this wall hanging was inspired by the vintage block as well. This is one of the quilts I made for Mary Kerr's book, *Quilt Block Challenge— Vintage Revisited*. Setting the label in the corner under the binding makes it a little more secure.

This was the fourth quilt I created for the "Vintage Revisited" challenge. I used the block we were given to make the accent border and the corner blocks on my quilt. These blocks are called Hen and Chicks, which inspired not only the center of the quilt, but also the egg-shaped labels. The label on the right records the title of the quilt, information on the challenge, who made it, and when. The label on the left records the process I went through designing my quilt and the techniques I used. To add just a hint of color, I drew red dots around the edges of the egg labels with a permanent fabric pen. I also could have used red embroidery floss and the outline stitch.

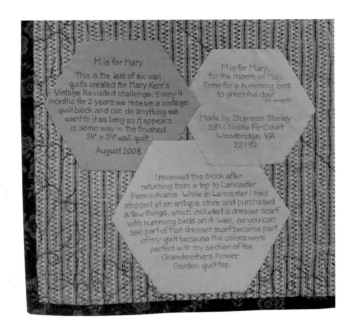

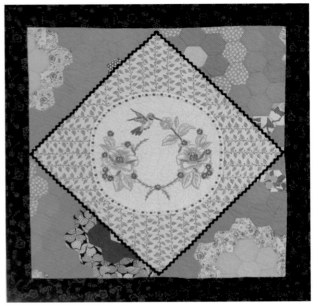

M is for Mary is the last of six quilts I made for the "Vintage Revisited" challenge. We were each given a piece of a Grandmother's Flower Garden quilt top, which is all made from small hexagons. I chose to make three assorted sizes and colors of hexagons to use for my labels on this wall hanging. The blue label records the title of the quilt, information about the challenge, and when the quilt was made. The pink label records a poem my mother wrote about the quilt, my name, and address. The green label includes information on the inspiration for this quilt.

One Lucky Clover
made in Spring 2010
by Shannon Shirley

This design is now my
R is for Rabbit pattern!

R is for RABBIT

Shamrocks are free motion quilted around the border
on this quilt. For luck, I also included one four-leaf clover.
The title of the quilt, *One Lucky Clover*, inspired the label.

The idea for the flower labels came from the theme of the first national quilt show this piece competed in. "What If" was the theme and my statement was: "What if we all stopped and smelled the flowers, listened to the birds sing, and maybe even played in the mud." I named my quilt *Stop and Smell the Flowers*. The flower labels record information about the class where I started the quilt, the photograph that inspired it, and the quilt's name, my name, and the date it was completed. The photograph is the picture I took of Dottie, a pig at the fair that inspired my quilt. The green label is the quilted ear tag Dottie wore when she was competing in the county and state fair because I felt she should be properly accessorized. Dottie won so many ribbons, I have to add another pair of leaves on the bottom left, so that I can record her prizes.

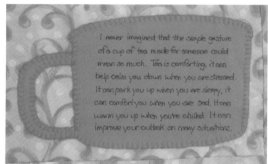

Simple Gesture is a small wall hanging I made for a quilt challenge with the theme "Reflections." I chose to reflect on the simple gesture of sharing a cup of tea with someone and what it has come to mean to me. The blue tea cups were my dad's favorite. The simple, solid blue shape worked well for this project and certainly connected the meaning of this quilt to the theme. One label explains the challenge and one label shares the words that are quilted in the background of the quilt, which are part of a much longer writing I did after going through some very difficult losses in my life.

I now share my website on the labels of my quilts that will travel. I hope that if someone wants to find out more about me that this will make it easy to contact me. Maybe they will want to hire me to lecture or teach or maybe they will want to purchase my quilt; you never know what will happen!

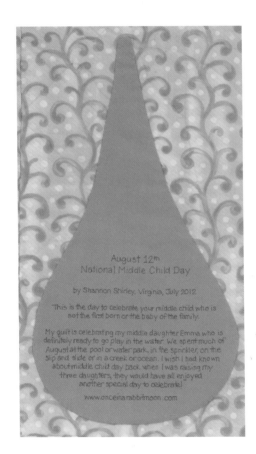

August 12th
National Middle Child Day

by Shannon Shirley, Virginia, July 2012

This is the day to celebrate your middle child who is
not the first born or the baby of the family.

My quilt is celebrating my middle daughter Emma who is
definitely ready to go play in the water. We spent much of
August at the pool or water park, in the sprinkler, on the
slip and slide or in a creek or ocean. I wish I had known
about middle child day back when I was raising my
three daughters, they would have all enjoyed
another special day to celebrate!

www.onceinarabbitmoon.com

All the blue fabrics in the background of this quilt represent the variety of water-related activities we loved to do during the summers when my girls were young. I decided to make a huge drop of water for the label, which was simple but relates to the quilt quite well.

The carrot labels are a design element from the front of the quilt. I even used the same three-dimensional torn, raw edge greens on the carrots.

December 2nd - National Mutt Day by Shannon Shirley, Virginia, May 2012

National Mutt Day is about embracing, saving and celebrating mixed breed dogs!
Millions of mixed breed dogs are waiting to be adopted today.
Once you go Mutt... you'll never go back!

www.onceinarabbitmoon.com   www.facebook.com/onceinarabbitmoon

PROUD TO BE A
MUTT

The idea for this label came from the backing fabric on this wall hanging. What dog doesn't love a bone? I should note on this label that Gilbert Delery was the model for the picture I drew. He is a Basset Bloodhound mix, and proud of it!

Chapter 5

Other Ways To Label Your Quilts

In this chapter I will share other methods I have used to make labels…

- Embroider on the label or the quilt.
- Use extra blocks, vintage or new.
- Write on the front or the back of the quilt or sleeve.
- Computer printed, with or without photos.

Hand embroidery certainly takes more time than using pen and ink, but it is beautiful! This tree skirt was a collaboration between my mum and I, so this family-tradition piece definitely deserved a special label. My mum did all the embroidery on this quilt and label; I did the piecing, quilting, and binding.

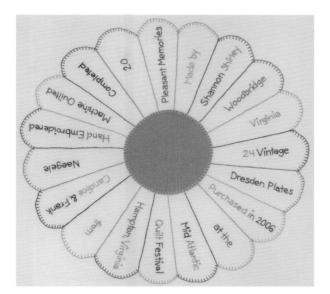

Here, the label is on the front of the quilt. In 2006, I bought twenty-four vintage Dresden Plate blocks. There are twelve each of two different sets, but the fabrics looked good together, so I decided to make a quilt for my bed. With a plan for five rows of five blocks, I was one block short. I hand-embroidered all the plates onto white squares, so I decided to embroider a Dresden Plate label to place in the center of the top row of the quilt. I got ahead of myself and sewed 2009 as the completion date. I picked 09 out in 2011 and will wait to finish the whole top, including borders, before I embroider the actual completion date.

Working with vintage blocks has always been one of my favorite sources of inspiration. Using extra blocks is a great way to coordinate the label.

For this challenge, we were given a vintage block (the blue star and solid blue background), a short piece of royal blue rick rack, and a few buttons. I chose to pick the star out of the center of the block and create three more stars for the front of the quilt. I replaced the blue print star with solid white fabric to create the label. I used a variety of colored fabric pens to create a label that coordinated with the mixed colors of this wall hanging.

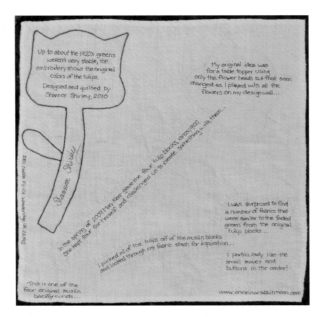

Up to about the 1920's greens weren't very stable, the embroidery shows the original colors of the tulips.

Designed and quilted by Shannon Shirley, 2010

My original idea was for a table topper using only the flower heads but that soon changed as I played with all the flowers on my design wall...

I was surprised to find a number of fabrics that were similar to the faded green from the original tulip blocks...

In the spring of 2009 Mary Kerr gave me four tulip blocks from 1910. She kept four for herself and challenged us to create something with them.

I picked all of the tulips off of the muslin blocks and looked through my fabric stash for inspiration...

I particularly like the small leaves and buttons in the center!

This is one of the four original muslin backgrounds...

www.onceinarabbitmoon.com

After receiving four vintage blocks and being challenged to create something unique with them, I picked all the appliqué pieces off of the muslin backgrounds. To retain the history of the original blocks, I used one of the backgrounds as the label for my Christmas tree skirt. I noted everything I knew about them into various spaces marked by the needle holes left in the fabric. I embroidered around one of the tulips shapes in the same colors of the thread that had been used to sew the appliqué pieces before the green faded so dramatically.

Another "Vintage Revisited" challenge piece and another background used as a label is displayed here. For this label, I marked the needle holes with a permanent fabric pen so that they could be more easily seen. I also quilted the label to the back of the wall hanging, being careful to only go into the batting and not through to the front of the quilt.

After creating this wall hanging for my parents, I used one of the leftover nine patches to make the label. I sewed cream-colored half-square triangles to each side of the nine patch to create a block similar to the ones on the quilt front. The information on this label includes where the vintage blocks were purchased, who the quilt was made for, who made the quilt, and when it was made, along with a thank you to my parents.

I love how this label turned out. I removed the center from a vintage block and replaced it with muslin. I used navy blue blanket stitching to sew down the edges. To add interest, I doodled a butterfly and a flower in some of the blank space left on the label.

As with vintage blocks, you can use extra blocks from newly pieced projects for labels. My guild had a block of the month drawing and my mum and I won the snowmen blocks. After I finished designing and piecing the quilt top, another guild member turned in her snowmen blocks. I combined those along with a leftover snowball block to create this label.

Another label option is to incorporate the label information right into a block on the front of the quilt.

Every block in this quilt has text written in it. Signatures from family members, along with their birth dates and places of birth fill most of the blocks. I added information about the celebration onto a couple of the remaining blocks. These blocks were all signed before the quilt was pieced.

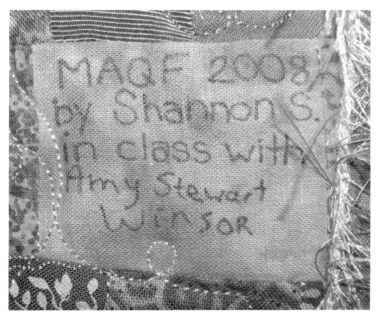

Sometimes when I am really short on time or energy, I write the information on the front of the quilt in an inconspicuous place or color. This is similar to an artist signing his or her work.

There are also times that I write the information on the back of the quilt or on the sleeve of the quilt.

These are both examples of small series I worked on. I wanted to identify the various techniques I used for each quilt so that I would remember, and so that when I used them as samples in my classes, my students could easily see the techniques used for each piece.

You need to remember that sleeves can be removed, just like labels, so the identification is not permanent. However, I have always thought that any of these methods are better than no identification at all.

These quilts and labels are from classes I took. I often write on the front or the back of a quilt during class so that I don't lose track of information about the class. I make notes on the date or place I took the class, the instructor's name, products and techniques used, and whether I used a provided pattern. This is important because as the years pass and you take more classes, it becomes more difficult to remember the details.

I have to admit that I am slower than some to convert to modern technology. Throughout my years of quilting, I have tried using my computer and printer to make labels. Personally, I would get frustrated for one reason or another and go back to making the labels by hand. As time passed and new products came out, I would occasionally try again with better results. Practicing with computer generated labels will reduce stress and frustration. Experiment until you find the method and products that work for you. As new products are developed, there will be more to learn.

Jenny's Cottage

I purchased this vintage embroidery years ago. In 2006 I chose fabrics and bordered the piece of needlework. In March 2008 I free motion quilted it and finally was able to hang it up and enjoy it.

By Shannon Shirley

Endless shades of text colors is one of the things I like the most about computer-printed labels. The huge number of fonts that are available these days could make some very interesting labels. Being able to plan the layout and see exactly what it will look like is helpful, and there certainly won't be any handwritten mistakes like I have made even when tracing the preprinted layout. I like the creativity of working by hand, however, copyright-free clip art can be added to a computer-generated label if you are not comfortable with hand drawing.

When you print a label, it is best to plan a whole page layout of a few of them so that you use the whole sheet of prepared-for-printing fabric, or make one very large label. The sheets are pricey, so not wasting any is your best plan.

No Maintenance Necessary

I made the postcards for a guild exchange in September 2005. They were the first postcards I had ever made and I couldn't part with all of them so in December I mounted them in a no maintenance fish tank.

By Shannon Shirley

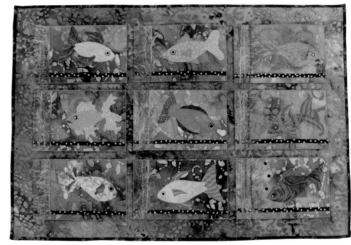

Many of the prepared-for-printing fabrics that I have used have been very stiff, so turning the edges under and sewing through the edge has not been easy or very professional looking. Check around and find those that maintain a soft hand and are machine washable, especially if the label is going on a quilt that will be cuddled and washed regularly.

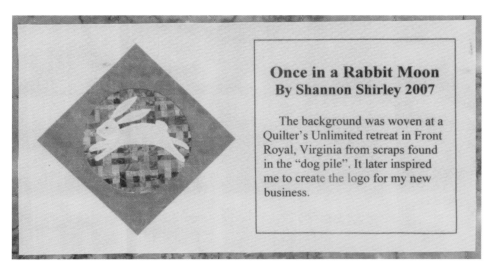

Once in a Rabbit Moon
By Shannon Shirley 2007

The background was woven at a Quilter's Unlimited retreat in Front Royal, Virginia from scraps found in the "dog pile". It later inspired me to create the logo for my new business.

Creating fusible labels using the printed fabrics is a good option for art quilts that won't be washed because they won't peel off over time. This one is raw edge, but the fusible keeps it from fraying. It is not a very finished look, but it certainly gets the job done.

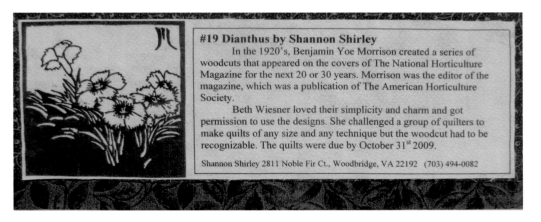

#19 Dianthus by Shannon Shirley

In the 1920's, Benjamin Yoe Morrison created a series of woodcuts that appeared on the covers of The National Horticulture Magazine for the next 20 or 30 years. Morrison was the editor of the magazine, which was a publication of The American Horticulture Society.

Beth Wiesner loved their simplicity and charm and got permission to use the designs. She challenged a group of quilters to make quilts of any size and any technique but the woodcut had to be recognizable. The quilts were due by October 31st 2009.

Shannon Shirley 2811 Noble Fir Ct., Woodbridge, VA 22192 (703) 494-0082

Being able to incorporate original illustrations is a useful option. In addition, on labels where you have quite a bit of information to record, you don't have to trace it all by hand and you can make the font smaller to keep the label size smaller. If I had handwritten this label, it would have been much bigger because my handwriting needs to be larger to be legible.

This preprinted label was given to anyone who participated in Beth Wiesner's "Block of the Month." She hand-wrote the label and then photocopied it to muslin that had been ironed to freezer paper. I signed my name and added additional information around the edge of the label. I added running stitch to represent the wind and snow blowing around, which gave the label some texture and held it down to the backing of the quilt.

This quilt is based on the design of the First Ladies Water Garden at the United States Botanical Gardens in Washington, D.C. The shape of the label is the silhouette of the garden's logo. A computer-printed label is great when you want to record a lot of information. While the shaped label connects to the front of the quilt, it was not my best idea. The prepared-for-printing fabric was very stiff, so turning the edges under was difficult. It would have been easier to fuse the tulip shape onto a square of the matching backing fabric and then machine stitch the edge of it, using a blanket, satin, or zigzag stitch before attaching it to the quilt. This would have given a much more professional look.

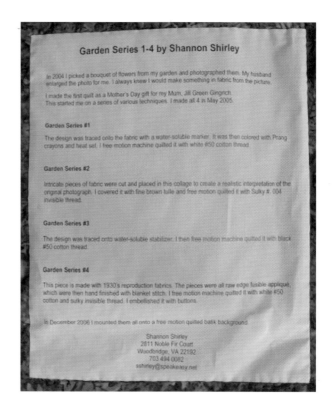

Each of the four small quilts in the photo were made as individual wall hangings, and each of them has a handwritten label attached to the back. At one point I basted them to the quilted green batik panel, so that I could enter them as one unit in a number of exhibits. Due to time restrictions, I printed the series of descriptions onto one sheet of prepared-for-printing fabric. This particular brand was very stiff and I now know that I could have machine sewn strips of fabric around the edge of this label and turned the edges of that under before stitching it to the back of the panel. I think including a fabric-printed copy of the original photograph I worked from would have added some color and interest to this label.

This full sheet label is better in a number of ways. First, the fabric is much softer as products have improved over the years. Second, it includes my photograph of the tulips that started this whole group project. Each section of this quilt was made by a different person. I had attached a separate label to all seven sections because they were planned to be returned to the artists after the project was done traveling. Because of the number of labels I was making and the amount of information I was recording, I decided to print the labels. In the end, each of the artists gifted me their section so that the quilts could remain together and travel with me for lectures. The artists retain visiting privileges.

Noah's Ark
Made by Shannon Shirley for the MDQPN 2010 Challenge "Two by Two"
The original artwork was created by my oldest daughter when she was five. It
was to hang in the nursery of our new baby who was born Oct. 22, 1991.

Shannon Shirley 2811 Noble Fir Ct. Woodbridge, Virginia 703 494-0082
www.onceinarabbitmoon.com

It was very important for me to include a photograph of the original artwork that inspired this quilt. I chose to mount this label upside down on the back of this wall hanging so that when someone turned the bottom edge up to look for a label, the drawing would be right-side up. I outline stitched around the edge of this label, which camouflages the bumpy stiff edge (this label was made before I learned about sewing strips of soft fabric around the edge of the label first). I am happy with the frame of red around the label.

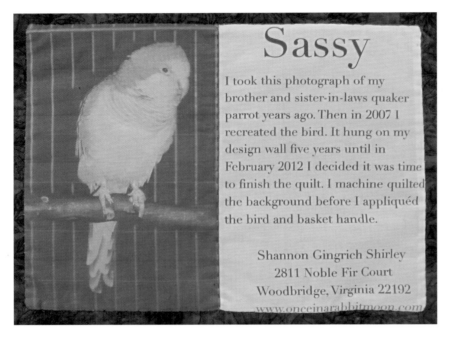

Sassy

I took this photograph of my brother and sister-in-laws quaker parrot years ago. Then in 2007 I recreated the bird. It hung on my design wall five years until in February 2012 I decided it was time to finish the quilt. I machine quilted the background before I appliquéd the bird and basket handle.

Shannon Gingrich Shirley
2811 Noble Fir Court
Woodbridge, Virginia 22192
www.onceinarabbitmoon.com

Sassy is the last photo label I made before I learned about the addition of soft fabric edges. I do love having the original photograph attached to the quilt. I should have reduced the size or the text part of this label so that there was a little more space around the edges. Cropping it so closely looks like I trimmed the label too small. I chose to stitch down the center line of the label, being careful not to go through to the front of the quilt.

I hope the variety of techniques and shapes of labels have inspired you to get creative with the labels for your quilts.

Chapter 6

Making Labels: Techniques and Tips

As I have already mentioned, the most important information to label your quilts with is your name and when it was made. Here is a list of other types of information to consider including:

- Who designed the quilt? Is it original, an adaptation, or a purchased pattern?
- Who worked on the quilt? The piecer and the quilter might be different people.
- Why was the quilt made? Was it a challenge, a celebration, or inspired by something in particular?
- Who was it made for? Was it a gift?
- Where was it made? Possibly, it was a round robin, made in different states or countries.
- What techniques were used to create the quilt, and were any special products used?
- Were the materials used vintage or new, and where did you acquire them?
- Are there stories about events that happened while making the quilt?

- Are there fabric-printed photos of anything pertaining to the quilt?
- Your name and address are often required if the quilt will be traveling to exhibits.
- Who taught the class, and when and where was it held?
- How should someone take care of the quilt (if you will not be keeping it)?
- What are the quilt's dimensions? (Often required when showing a piece.)
- Has the quilt been exhibited in shows, juried into any competitions, or won any awards? You may want to add this information to existing labels or make another label as the need arises.

Now we are going to get into making the labels to record this information on!

When I first started making labels, I would just write and draw directly on the fabric and hope not to make mistakes. My next step was to pre-write the label information on paper and then rewrite it on the fabric. The problem that arose from this method was that it was difficult for me to keep the lines straight, which I found frustrating. Often I would end up redoing the label and throwing the first one in the trash. As I became more comfortable with computers, I started preparing the text using a basic word-processing program. Typically, I set the font size at 18 points, centered, so that the layout of the label was even and straight. I could reword it and move it around easily and see exactly how it would look. After I was happy with the wording and layout, I would print a copy of it. Using a sunny window or a light box, I would trace the words onto the fabric using a permanent Micron® pen.

Steps to create a basic label:

1. Prepare text using an 18-point font, centered. (You can make it larger or smaller, this is just the size I use.)
2. Print a copy of the text on paper.
3. Trace the text onto the fabric using a Micron® pen. (I use size .05.)
4. Heat set the ink with a hot, dry iron.
5. Use the method of your choice to finish label. (I will share these options later in this chapter.)

This is the first of six wall quilts created
for Mary Kerr's 2 year challenge
Every 4 months we receive a vintage
quilt block and can do anything we want
to it as long as it appears in some way in
the finished 24" x 24" wall quilt.

Made by Shannon Shirley
August 2006
Virginia

Prepared text, printed on paper.

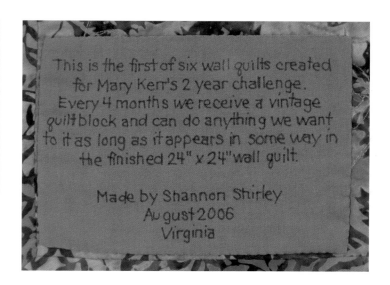

Traced onto fabric using a light box and a Micron pen.

QPN
Challenge, 2012
Vintage embroidered blocks
distributed March 2011 by Mary Kerr.
Create an 18" wall hanging using
the block in some way.
by Shannon Shirley
Virginia

If I know what shape label I am making, I can adjust the length of each line so that they gradually increase and decrease to fit that shape.

For instance, if I want to make a square on point, I begin by preparing the text. The length of each line is good, but it still isn't a square, so I increased the size of the lines. I did not change the font size.

QPN

Challenge, 2012

Vintage embroidered blocks

distributed March 2011 by Mary Kerr.

Create an 18" wall hanging using

the block in some way.

by Shannon Shirley

Virginia

You can see that this is much more likely to fit in a square on point. The first layout looks more like a diamond. After you are happy with the layout you can trace it onto the fabric using a permanent fabric pen in whatever color you choose.

Most of the time I like to use my own handwriting instead of tracing the exact font I have printed, but occasionally, I will use a special font for the title of the quilt or, in the case of the label shown here, the logo from the Arts and Old Lace challenge.

Additional Points to Remember:

Directions are the same regardless of what shape of label you are making. We'll start with basic labels.

I have traced the words before and after sewing the labels. Just remember that if you trace the text afterwards, you may have to remake the whole label if you make a mistake.

Most of my early labels were white or beige muslin and often the backing fabric of the quilt showed through the label. This could be alleviated by using a double layer of fabric. You could choose to press the two layers' edges under, but this seems like it would be difficult. A preferred method might be to iron a fusible product to a piece of material. Cut out a piece the finished size of the label you want. Peel off the paper and fuse it to the back of the label you have traced, carefully centering it on the text. Trim a quarter inch around the fused shape and press the seam allowance to the back side of the label. This method would keep the backing fabric from showing through, but it would also make the label stiff. My preferred method is turned edge with interfacing or fabric, which I will explain in this chapter.

Pressed Edge Labels were the first type I made and I really disliked this method. I usually burned the tips of my fingers while trying to press a neat quarter-inch seam allowance all the way around the edge. If the label had corners, I struggled to get an accurate 90-degree mitered corner. If it was curved, I struggled to get a smooth curve.

If you choose this method, cut out your label with an additional quarter-inch seam allowance and press the raw edges to the back of the label. If necessary you can use starch to make the pressed edges crisper, but this will make them harder to hand stitch through.

Use the blind stitch to attach the label to the back of the quilt using thread that blends with the label fabric.

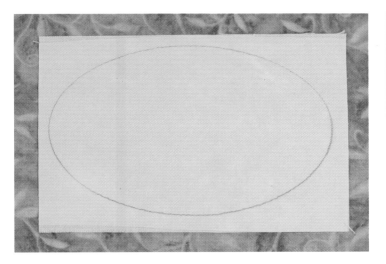
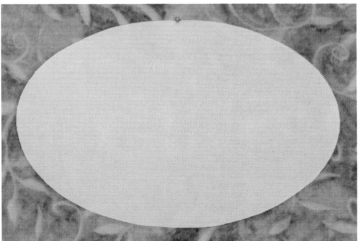

Making *Solid Fusible* raw edge labels is easy. Trace the shape you want your label to be onto Heat-n-Bond Lite®. Check to see that the text fits into the traced shape by placing the fusible paper over the printed text. Iron this piece of paper-backed fusible to the back of the label fabric. Cut out the label on the traced pencil line. Peel off the paper backing and iron into place on the back of the quilt. This type of label will be stiffer than a label without fusible. If the quilt is one that is going to be washed, you need to stitch down the raw edge of the label. I use hand blanket stitching. If you want to attach a fused label by machine, you will have to do this before you layer the quilt back with the batting and quilt front, otherwise you will be stitching through all three layers and it will show on the front.

For *Window Fusible*, trace the shape of your label onto the paper side of your fusible product. Before ironing it to the back of your label fabric, use a craft blade or small detail scissors to cut away the center of the shape, leaving approximately one-quarter inch inside the traced pencil lines. Iron the fusible product onto the back of the label fabric and cut out the shape on the traced pencil lines.

Peel off the thin strip of paper on the back of the label to expose the fusible product.

Following the product guidelines, iron the label to the back of the quilt. Again, I choose to finish the edge of these labels with hand blanket stitch. This type of label will have a soft hand, as the fusible is only a thin line around the edge of the label.

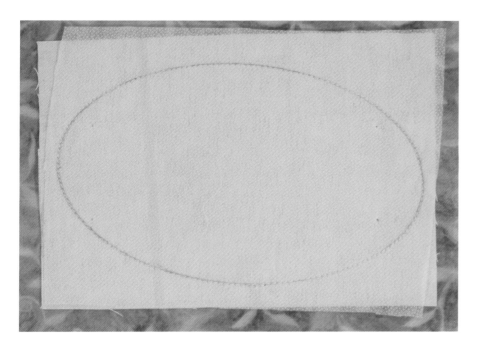

My favorite method for making labels is *Turned Edge with Interfacing.* The directions are as follows:

1. Trace or draw finished size and shape of label onto lightweight interfacing. If using lightweight fusible interfacing, draw on the fusible side.
2. Place the interfacing with the traced shape on the front of the label fabric and stitch on the pencil line you drew. I usually use a slightly smaller stitch than normal because it makes turning curves easier.

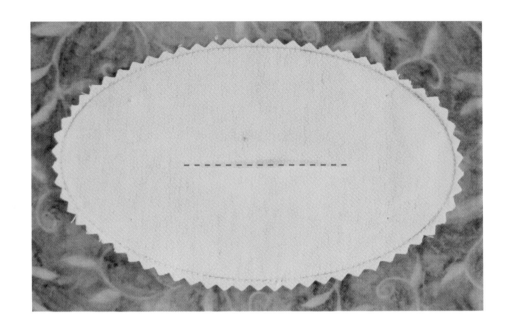

3. Trim around the edge of the label using pinking shears.
4. Carefully cut a small slit in the interfacing only, approximately two inches long.

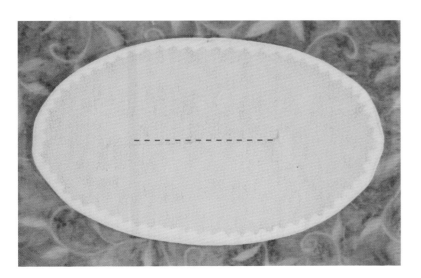

Press the finished edges carefully.

5. Gently turn the label right side out. Using a tool helps make this process easier.

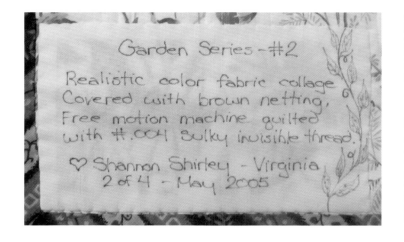

Turned Edge with Fabric would be my method of choice to alleviate the shadowing of the backing fabric.

Making this type of label is the same as *Turned Edge With Interfacing,* but uses fabric instead of interfacing, so that the label is double thick and the edges are nicely turned.

Additional Points to Remember:

Follow the directions on the fusible product you are using because all brands have slightly different directions.

If you are using fusible lightweight interfacing, draw on the fusible side (often the side that is just slightly bumpy) and sew with this side facing up, so that when you trim and turn your label and get ready to press, it fuses to the back side of the label and not the ironing board.

If you are fusing your label and the shape of your label isn't symmetrical, remember to trace your shape in reverse so the shape faces the correct direction.

Use permanent fabric pens like Micron® to write the text because they are very fine pens and don't bleed much. I like the .05 size best. I find the tips of the smaller ones get caught on the threads of the material and the larger one makes a heavy line especially when brand new.

For decorating labels, I use a variety of permanent fabric markers, like Fabrico®, Marvy®, and Fabricmate®.

Here are some other tips for labeling your quilts.

Use leftover appliqué pieces to embellish your label.

Fussy cut and fuse pieces of fabrics in the quilt to create a coordinating label.

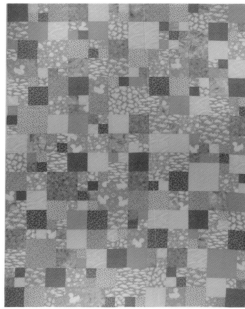

Fussy cut whole motifs from novelty prints to use as labels.

Border stiff computer-printed pictures or labels with fabric for a more polished look and to make the label easier to attach.

Tucking the label under the binding makes it a little bit more secure, but if someone wanted to remove it they could with not much effort. Adding a photograph printed on prepared-for-printing fabric sheets would be an interesting addition to this quilt's story. Adding a description of the vacation I was on and who I was with would also have been a good idea, but I was in a hurry to use this piece for a class sample so the label was very minimal. You can always go back and add more.

Fusible applique, hand embroidery.

Thankful...
Recreated by Shannon Shirley, Virginia Spring 2011
machine quilting Bernina 1130, beaded!

Original artwork by Emma Shirley
Second Grade
Age 7
1995

www.onceinarabbitmoon.com

thankful

This label technique is the quickest and easiest for me to make. You cut a square of fabric and press it in half diagonally. Tuck it into the corner before binding the quilt and stitch down the folded edge. The more information you want to write, the larger the square you cut. It's that easy!

If you want to fuse your label, but you also want it to be sewn down, fuse it to fabric that matches the backing fabric of the quilt. Then make a basic shape label and hand stitch it to the back of the quilt. If you stitch it to the quilt backing before you layer and quilt it, you will probably quilt through the label, which is fine unless you don't like the look.

Raw edge fusible labels are okay on wall quilts that will not be washed. This label was given to everyone who exhibited a quilt at our guild's show in 2008. I fussy cut around the edge of the picture before fusing it to the back of the quilt.

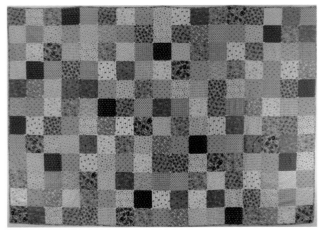

On this quilt, I not only put a label on it, but one of the squares is a pocket. Inside the pocket is the note I wrote to my daughter on fabric using permanent fabric markers. I drew all kinds of pictures and wrote down special things I wanted her to remember if she traveled with her quilt. One thing I need to do is attach a piece of ribbon or rick rack to the note and stitch the other end inside the pocket so it cannot get lost.

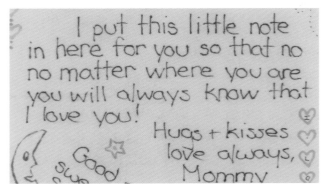

Free motion quilt your name and the date right into the
quilt in matching thread if you really want it to blend in.

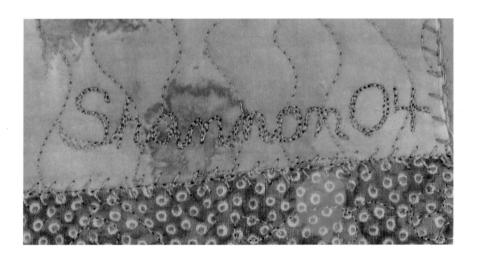

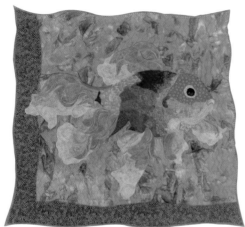

Choosing a contrasting thread color and sewing over it multiple times will make it stand out.

If someone tried to pick this out of the quilt, it would likely still show up, making it possible to identify if the quilt is stolen.

Chapter 7

Simple Details, Big Difference

Little details can make such a difference in the look of a label. Sometimes when a project has to be finished right away, a basic label might be all you have time for. As you will see in this chapter, if you are short on time you can add a simple label and think about embellishing it later when things slow down a bit. I think you will agree it makes a big difference.

Instead of just basting an address label on a quilt, think about taking the extra five to ten minutes to make an oval label with turned edges; it looks so much more professional.

Tracing the outline of the sunflower from the original drawing that my youngest daughter Jenny had made years ago certainly made this label coordinate with the quilt. I used a permanent fabric marker to get the heavier black line of the flower before tracing the words with a permanent fabric pen. Adding a variety of small black buttons not only held the label down better, but I think it adds a bit more interest. The front of the quilt had white buttons on the sunflowers, so it carries a similar design element to the label. Embroidering the picture using outline stitch would have been even nicer.

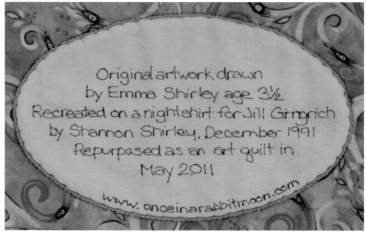

Plain labels can be improved by adding an accent color around the edge of the label. In this case, orange set it off from the background. I could not add blanket stitch because that would have covered the website information that I had already written on the label. I looked to see if I had any orange rick rack that I could embellish it with, but I only had medium and I needed mini, so that it didn't overpower the size of the label. I settled on hand-embroidered outline stitch using all six strands of floss, which I think ended up working out well.

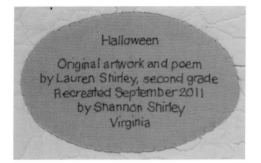

This is another label that I decided needed a little more attention. I considered rick rack, but when I found the extra spider button, I decided to use the outline stitch and continue the stitched line down into the label and sew the spider button hanging from it. The label was fine like this, but I decided to go ahead and add the baby rick rack and it's even better now!

This label was fine with the two colors of text, but the space at the top bothered me, so I decided to add a double-star button tied on with embroidery floss, like the buttons on the front of the quilt. To finish it off, I did a running stitch around the outer edge of the label using six stands of floss. When you do this running stitch, you need to be careful to not stitch through to the front of the quilt. I like to stitch into the batting because it gives the label texture like it has been quilted.

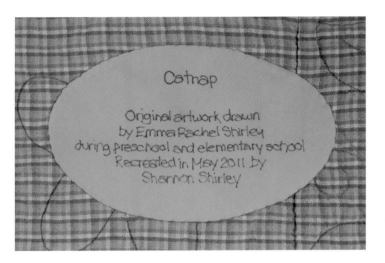

On this particular label, I considered drawing paw prints walking all the way around the label, but when I found a rubber stamp of a paw print, I decided to use it instead. The stamp was too big to fit all around the edge, so I did a row of running stitch using two strands of floss and then stamped paw prints beside the title of the quilt. I used a permanent fabric marker to ink the stamp and then touched it up a little with a permanent fabric pen.

Free To Be Me! is a very colorful quilt, so I chose to add blanket stitch using two strands of variegated floss. I like the frame it gives the label and it makes it seem more secure, even though someone could pick out all the stitching and remove it if they really wanted to.

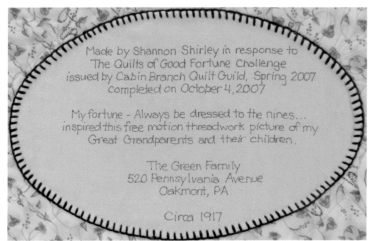

Blanket stitching around this label using six strands of floss framed it out nicely. There was a small dark brown accent border on the quilt front, so I used that color floss on the label to coordinate.

Occasionally, the labels may bleed when they are washed. You should always set the inks with a dry hot iron just to be sure, even if the directions for the brand of pens you are using don't require it.

When you are blanket stitching an outside corner, always remember to take an extra stitch in place to secure the corners so that they do not shift over time.

Sunflower #2

This quilt was inspired by original artwork drawn by Jenny Shirley while in the Third Grade. This piece is reduced to 50% of the original size and was made by Shannon Gingrich Shirley Virginia, August 2012.

Sunflower #2

This quilt was inspired by original artwork drawn by Jenny Shirley while in the Third Grade. This piece is reduced to 50% of the original size and was made by Shannon Gingrich Shirley Virginia, August 2012.

Making a yellow label to coordinate with the sunflowers was an easy choice. I embroidered around the label with purple floss, but decided it needed more of an accent. The purple trim from the inner border on the quilt top worked out much better.

Chapter 8

Hand Embroidery Stitches

Directions for left-handed people are on the following left pages.
Directions for right-handed people are on the following right pages.

Blanket stitch is my favorite embroidery stitch. It can be used to attach labels to your quilts when you want to add detail or color around the edge of your label.

Outline stitch (sometimes referred to as stem stitch) can be used to add a narrow line of accent color around your label or you can use it to embroider the entire label, including the text.

Running stitch can be used to add a colorful accent stripe on your label, or you can use matching thread and use this stitch to give the appearance of quilting.

Ninety-five percent of the time I use two strands of embroidery floss for any stitch I am working on. Occasionally, I adjust that number to achieve a particular look.

I have always loved hand embroidery. It is relaxing and it makes a great take-along project!

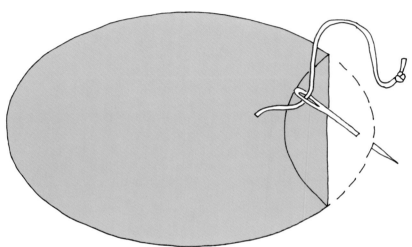

If you are left-handed you will stitch clockwise around your label starting on the right side.

Thread your needle with two strands of floss approximately 18 inches long.

Tie a knot about a quarter of an inch from the end of the floss.

Work with the label to your left and the backing fabric to your right.

Lift up the edge of the label and take a stitch into the backing fabric to secure the knot under the label (being careful not to go through to the front of the quilt).

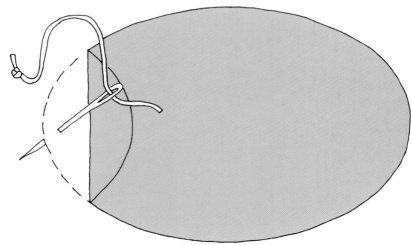

If you are right-handed, you will stitch counter-clockwise around your label starting on the left side.

Thread your needle with two strands of floss approximately 18 inches long.

Tie a knot about a quarter of an inch from the end of the floss.

Work with the label to your right and the backing fabric to your left.

Lift up the edge of the label and take a stitch into the backing fabric to secure the knot under the label (being careful not to go through to the front of the quilt).

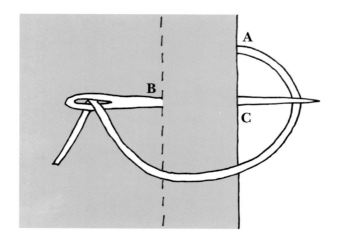

Bring the needle up just outside the edge of the label at (A).

Determine what size stitch you want to use and form an imaginary line. (I usually use 3/16 inch.)

Slide your needle down the side of the label and then in the same distance (to the imaginary dotted line).

In one movement, take a stitch from (B) to (C), making sure you do not go through to the front of the quilt.

Notice that the needle comes up and goes over the thread to the right.

I find it helps to use your right thumb to hold the thread down as you work.

When you pull the needle through to finish the stitch, it forms a reverse capital "L."

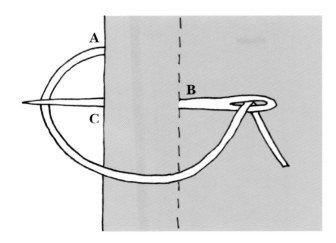

Bring the needle up just outside the edge of the label at (A).

Determine what size stitch you want to use and form an imaginary line. (I usually use 3/16 inch.)

Slide your needle down the side of the label and then in the same distance (to the imaginary dotted line).

In one movement, take a stitch from (B) to (C), making sure you do not go through to the front of the quilt.

Notice that the needle comes up and goes over the thread to the left.

I find it helps to use your left thumb to hold the thread down as you work.

When you pull the needle through to finish the stitch, it forms a capital L.

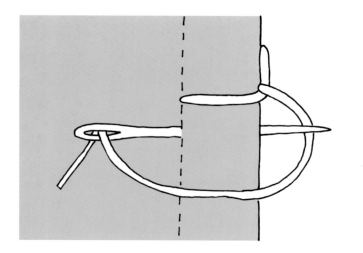

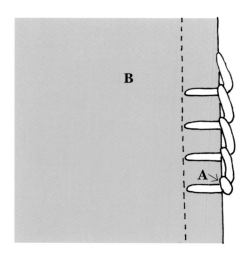

Continue to move your needle down the edge of your label and into the imaginary line to form your stitch size. This size may vary from project to project, but you want to try to keep them a regulated size as you stitch each label down.

As you continue to sew around your label you may run out of thread. Make a small half knot at the corner of your last reverse L stitch (A), and then carefully run your threads through the layers of your quilt, coming up inside the center of your label (B). Carefully trim the end of the thread so that the tail is hidden inside the layers. When you start a new thread, take a hidden stitch under the label to hide the knot and come up at the inside corner of last reverse L stitch that you took (A), and continue as before.

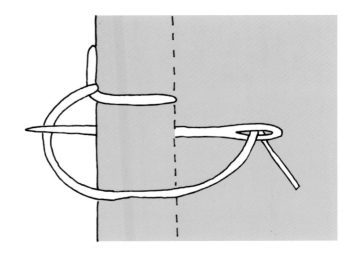

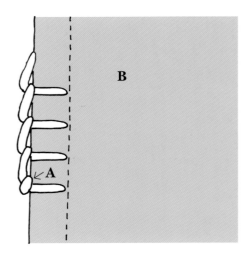

Continue to move your needle down the edge of your label and into the imaginary line to form your stitch size. This size may vary from project to project, but you want to try to keep them a regulated size as you stitch each label down.

As you continue to sew around your label, you may run out of thread. Make a small half-knot at the corner of your last "L" stitch (A) and then carefully run your threads through the layers of your quilt, coming up inside the center of your label (B). Carefully trim the end of the thread, so that the tail is hidden inside the layers. When you start a new thread, take a hidden stitch under the label to hide the knot and come up at the inside corner of the last "L" stitch that you took (A), and continue as before.

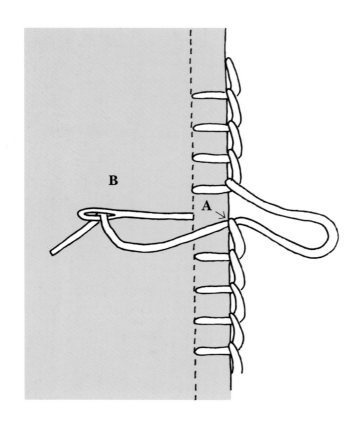

When you have stitched the entire way around your label and are back to the first reverse "L" stitch you made, slip your needle under the top edge of your first reverse L stitch (A).

Take your last stitch carefully, coming up close to (A) again.

Make a discreet half-knot at (A).

Carefully run your thread from (A) through the layers of your quilt, coming up inside the center of your label at (B).

Carefully trim the end of the thread at (B) so that the tail is hidden inside the layers.

When you have stitched the entire way around your label and are back to the first "L" you made, slip your needle under the top edge of your last "L" stitch (A).

Take your last stitch carefully, coming up close to (A) again.

Make a discreet half-knot at (A).

Carefully run your threads from (A) through the layers of your quilt, coming up inside the center of your label at (B).

Carefully trim the end of the thread at (B) so that the tail is hidden inside the layers.

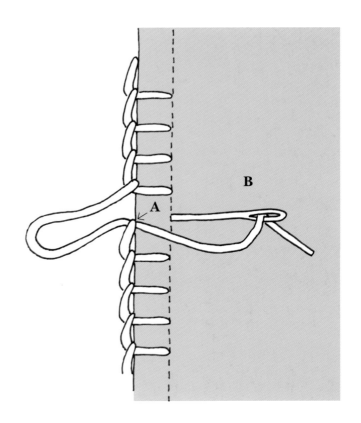

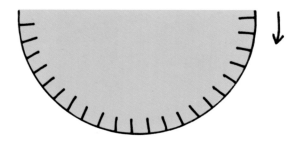

Outside Curve

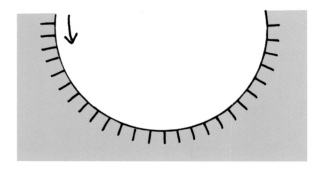

Inside Curve

When you use the blanket stitch, the most important detail besides regulating your stitch size is the angle of your stitches. You want to make each stitch to be as close to perpendicular to the edge of your label as you can.

As you move your way around a shape, you want to gradually change the angle of your stitches so that there are no obvious differences.

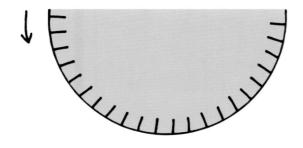

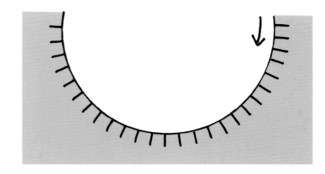

Outside Curve   Inside Curve

When you use the blanket stitch, the most important detail besides regulating your stitch size is the angle of your stitches. You want to make each stitch to be as close to perpendicular to the edge of your label as you can.

As you move your way around a shape, you want to gradually change the angle of your stitches so that there are no obvious differences.

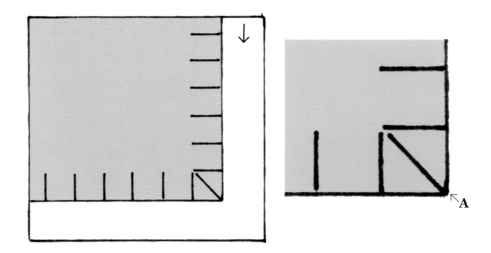

When you are going to stitch an outside 90-degree corner, you will be stitching around the label in a clockwise direction. As you get to the corner, adjust the spaces of your stitches so that they are fairly uniform as you turn the corner.

Rotate the angle of your stitch at the corner to a 45-degree angle.

Before you continue down the next side, take an extra stitch at the point to secure the corner stitch in place (A).

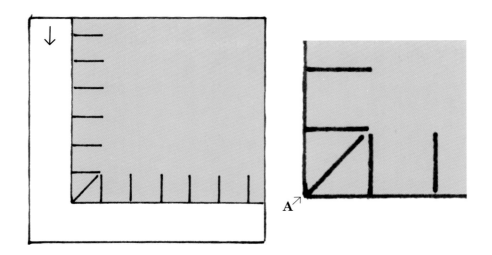

When you are going to stitch an outside 90-degree corner, you will be stitching around the label in a counter-clockwise direction. As you get to the corner, adjust the spaces of your stitches so that they are fairly uniform as you turn the corner.

Rotate the angle of your stitch at the corner to a 45-degree angle.

Before you continue down the next side take an extra stitch at the point to secure the corner stitch in place (A).

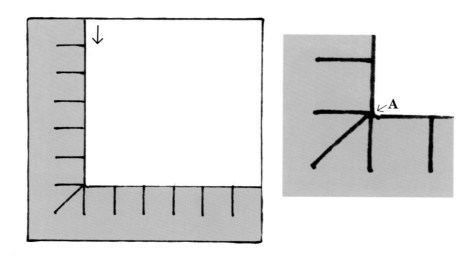

When you are stitching an inside 90-degree corner, you will be moving around the edge of the label in a clockwise direction.

Three stitches will pivot at the corner from the same spot (A).

There is no need to secure an inside corner, just continue around your label.

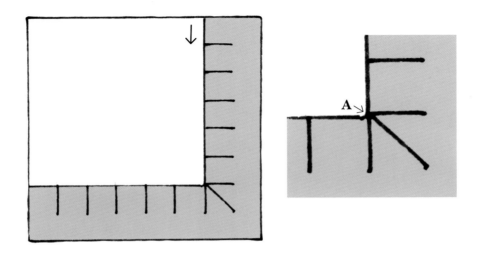

When you are stitching an inside 90-degree corner, you will be moving around the edge of the label in a counter-clockwise direction.

Three stitches will pivot at the corner from the same spot (A).

There is no need to secure an inside corner, just continue around your label.

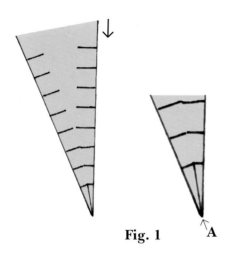

Fig. 1

A

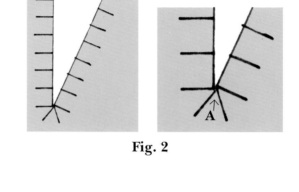

Fig. 2

When you are going to stitch an outside corner less than 90 degree, you will be stitching around the edge of the label in a clockwise direction. As you get to the corner, you will need to adjust the length of your stitches to fit the tiny space. **Fig.1**

Rotate the angle of your stitch at the corner.

Before you continue down the next side, take an extra stitch at the point (A) to secure the corner stitch in place.

When you are stitching an inside corner more than 90 degree, you will be moving around the edge of the label in a clockwise direction. **Fig. 2**

Fours stitches will pivot at the corner from the same spot (A).

There is no need to secure an inside corner, just continue around your label.

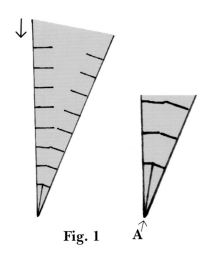

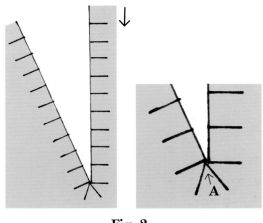

Fig. 1   A↗   **Fig. 2**

When you are going to stitch an outside corner less than 90-degree, you will be stitching counter-clockwise. As you get to the corner, you will need to adjust the length of your stitches to fit the tiny space. **Fig. 1**

Rotate the angle of your stitch at the corner.

Before you continue down the next side, take an extra stitch at the point (A) to secure the corner stitch in place.

When you are stitching an inside corner more than 90- degree, you will be moving around the label in a counter- clockwise direction. **Fig. 2**

Fours stitches will pivot at the corner from the same spot (A).

There is no need to secure an inside corner, just continue around your label.

You will work this stitch from the right to the left. Carefully hide your knot under the label or pull it through the fabric to the inside of the layers of the quilt. Depending on how thick of a line you want around the label, use anywhere from 2-6 strands of floss. (I almost always use 2 strands.)

Come up at (A).

In one movement, take a stitch by going in at (B) and out at (C.) **Fig. 1**

Continue in at (D) and out at (B.) In at (E) out at (D.)

In at (F) out at (E) until you come all the way around the label.

You will end by going in a (C.) **Fig. 2**

Come up somewhere along the edge and hide a half knot as discreetly as possible.

Travel through the layer a few inches to hide the tail of your thread and trim off the excess.

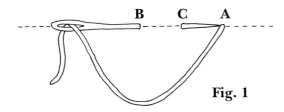

Fig. 1

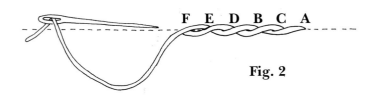

Fig. 2

You will work this stitch from the left to the right Carefully hide your knot under the label or pull it through the fabric to the inside of the layers of the quilt. Depending on how thick of a line you want around the label, use anywhere from 2-6 strands of floss. (I almost always use 2 strands.)

Come up at (A).

In one movement, take a stitch by going in at (B) and out at (C.) **Fig. 1**

Continue in at (D) and out at (B.) In at (E) out at (D.)

In at (F) out at (E) until you come all the way around the label.

You will to end by going in a (C.) **Fig. 2**

Come up somewhere along the edge and hide a half knot as discreetly as possible.

Travel through the layer a few inches to hide the tail of your thread and trim off the excess.

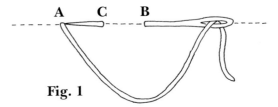

Fig. 1

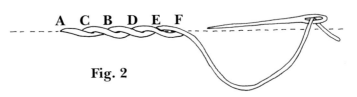

Fig. 2

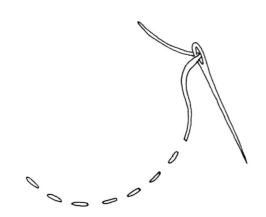

This stitch can be worked in straight or curved lines. Running stitches can vary in size depending on what look you are trying to achieve.

Work from left to right, keeping your stitches even.

To embellish or add texture to your label, work this stitch by passing the needle over and under the fabric.

You can take several evenly spaced stitches onto your needle at one time.

I like to stitch into the batting, but be careful not to go through to the front of the quilt.

Start with a piece of floss (2 strands), Perle cotton or quilting thread that is no longer than 18 inches.

Thread your needle and tie a knot about a quarter-inch from the end.

Carefully hide your knot under your label by coming in from the side or pulling your knot through like you would in quilting.

Do the same when you finish or run out of thread.

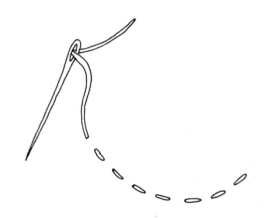

This stitch can be worked in straight or curved lines. Running stitches can vary in size depending on what look you are trying to achieve.

Work from right to left, keeping your stitches even.

To embellish or add texture to your label, work this stitch by passing the needle over and under the fabric.

You can take several evenly spaced stitches onto your needle at one time.

I like to stitch into the batting, but be careful not to go through to the front of the quilt.

Start with a piece of floss (2 strands), Perle cotton or quilting thread that is no longer than 18 inches.

Thread your needle and tie a knot about a quarter-inch from the end.

Carefully hide your knot under your label by coming in from the side or pulling your knot through, like you would in quilting.

Do the same when you finish or run out of thread.

My mum, Jill Green Gingrich, and I worked on this queen-sized quilt together. I pieced it and she hand-quilted it. We spent two years working on it and finished it in 1996. It has never had a label and it certainly deserves one. It would be a shame for this quilt's story to be lost. I would like future generations to know who made this quilt. I know my mum and I love finding names on old quilts we find!

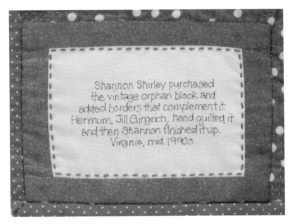

Shannon Shirley purchased
the vintage orphan block and
added borders that complement it.
Her mum, Jill Gingrich, hand quilted it
and then Shannon finished it up.
Virginia, mid 1990s

This quilt was inspired by a vintage orphan block I bought at a quilt show. I chose the fabrics and added two borders. My mum hand-quilted the entire piece and I finished it off with the green binding. We created this back in the mid-1990s. No one would ever know this without a label. In November 2012, while writing this book, I made a label for both of these quilts.

Every quilt deserves a label recording its story. Why not get creative and make it a pretty one! My hope is that I have inspired you to record your quilts' stories and that you might even enjoy doing it. Relax, have fun, and see what beautiful labels you can make!

Shapes to Trace

On the following pages, I have provided a series of graduated shapes for you to trace for making labels. I suggest if you find that you use one particular size and shape frequently, that you make a plastic template of it. This will make your job even easier and quicker. The horizontal dotted line is a reference guide to help you to line up your text before you trace it onto the label.

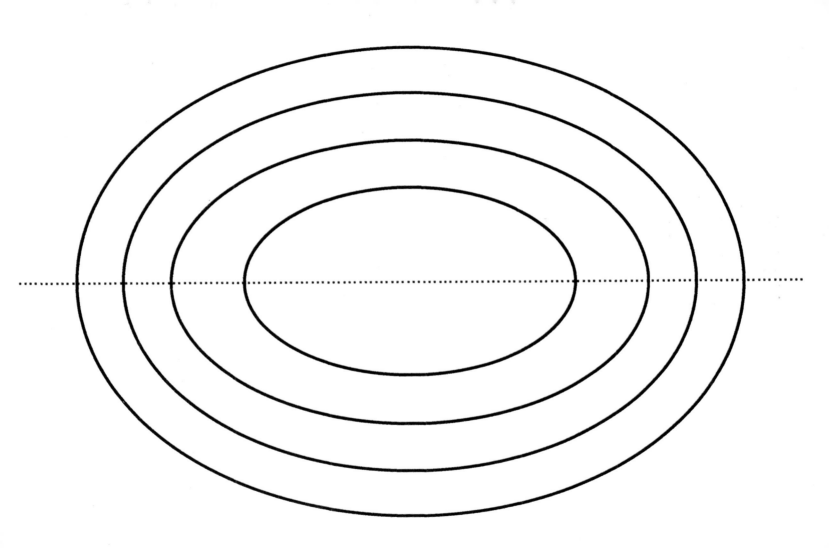

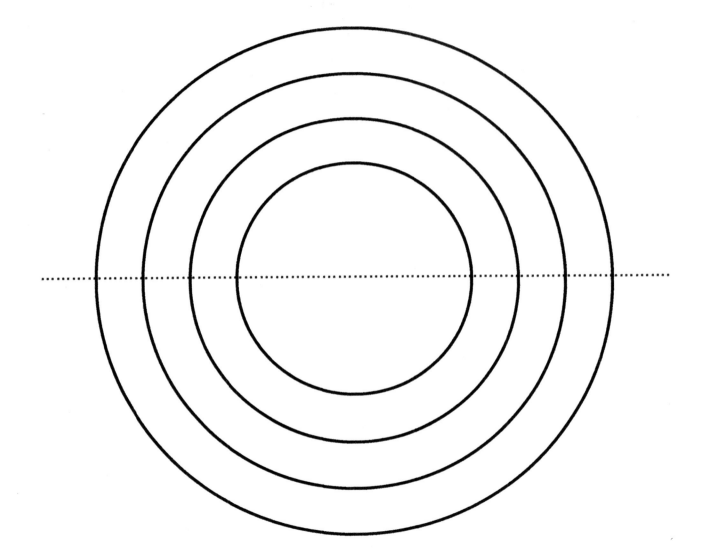

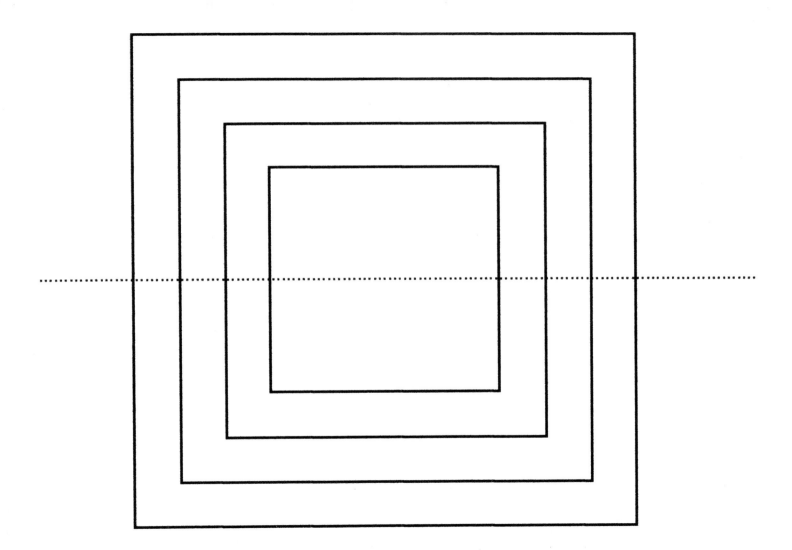

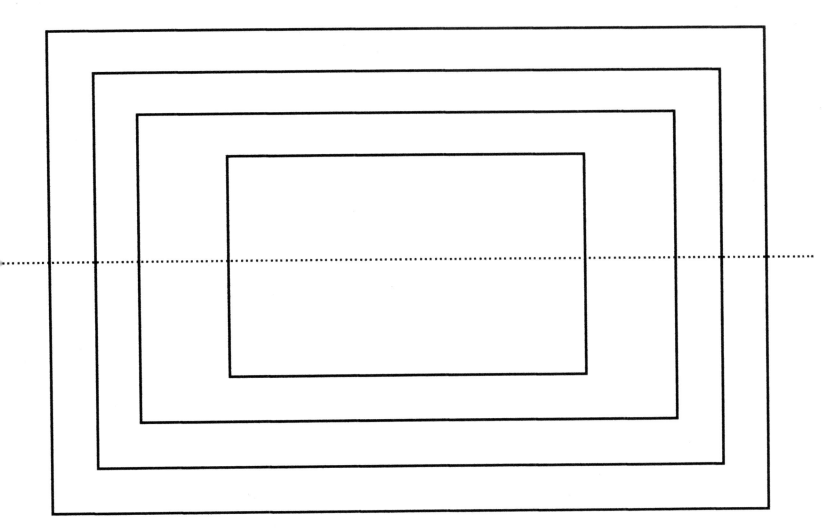